One Family, Two Views:

How to Fortify Your Mixed-Faith Mormon Marriage

By Natasha Helfer Parker, MS, LCMFT, CST,

Copyright @ 2018 Natasha Helfer Parker.

All rights reserved.

ISBN 978-1724860101

Dedication

To those who want to live in spaces where relationships are more important than beliefs. And especially to those within my own family unit, because it is my love for each of them that has helped me know this important truth.

Contents

Introduction   6

Chapter 1: Find Common Ground   9

Chapter 2: Avoid Unilateral Decisions   19

Chapter 3: Agree that You Both Have a Right to Parent Your Children   29

Chapter 4: Consider Anger Management and Displaced Anger   39

Chapter 5: See Your Mixed-Faith Marriage as an Asset   49

INTRODUCTION

When I start working with a couple who finds themselves in a mixed-faith marriage, I find that beneath the initial panic/discomfort/annoyance/anger (whatever emotion best fits for you) usually lies a basic fear about "our contract" being changed.

Comments I typically hear from the spouse who is not transitioning (or is transitioning less) include the following:

- I didn't sign up for this.
- I thought we had our goals and parenting style set. Now I have no idea what to expect from you.
- You keep changing the rules.
- I'm forced to face this only because of changes you're experiencing. It's not fair.
- I don't want our children's testimonies negatively impacted because of your new ways of seeing things.
- How could you have done this to us?

Things I typically hear from the transitioner:

- I never meant to hurt you or our family.
- I can't help what I feel.
- I can't believe you're not willing to talk about this with me or look into the things I've been reading and listening to.

- I feel so betrayed by my religion, and now you're turning against me too.
- I'm just supposed to stay silent with my own kids about my beliefs?
- It feels like you're choosing the church over me.

Although anyone who signs up for a 50- to 70-year monogamous journey should grasp that the contract is bound to evolve over time, not many things bring this reality into sharper focus than a faith transition of one or both spouses within Mormonism. The Mormon way of life includes so many expectations and "markers" that affect day-to-day life (not to mention the eternal perspective), it's easy to imagine why this is so.

Every Mormon marker is now under intense scrutiny: wearing garments, paying tithing, praying, studying the scriptures, holding Family Home Evening (and deciding what to teach), Word of Wisdom adherence, church attendance, callings, sex education of children, and so forth. It's very understandable that both spouses would feel overwhelmed by so many once-settled issues suddenly becoming unsettled. Distressing situations for both spouses are now coming up daily – negotiating the "settled" issues, processing new expectations, dealing with the uncertainties about what life going forward is going to look like.

I recently offered strategies for navigating this painful initial stage to members of a Facebook support group called *Mormon Mixed Faith Marriages*. I've compiled them into this book under five main topics:

1. Find common ground.
2. Avoid unilateral decisions.
3. Agree that you both have a right to parent your children.
4. Consider anger management and watch for displaced anger.
5. See your mixed-faith marriage as an asset.

Chapter 1
Find Common Ground

A first strategy for managing the initial stage of a mixed-faith marriage is to slow down and find common ground. How?

Understand that fear is a primary emotion that needs validation.

Fear is a primary emotion that gets masked by secondary emotions, mainly anger. It's hard to see your spouse as afraid when they're acting angry. Be willing to see your partner from the perspective of how afraid they must be. Validate your spouse's fear. Validation does not equal agreement. It simply reassures your spouse that you're listening and hearing and that you care about his or her distress.

Avoid seeing faith transition as an emergency.

When distressing emotions are high, it's tempting to rush through them toward relief. This approach doesn't work and often backfires. You have a lot of time to figure things out. Take all the time you need.

Faith transitions affect identity on many different levels and include many tasks. Give yourselves time to percolate the issues so you can avoid rash decisions. You don't need to make lifestyle changes in the first few months of a faith transition, especially if the transitioner waited a long time to disclose. The non-transitioning spouse needs time to adjust and make sense of new positions and beliefs. The believing spouse also need not make rash decisions, such as doubling down on religious observance.

Spiritual journeys are primarily personal.

Although you're a team, spiritual journeys are highly personal. As the parable of the 10 virgins teaches, we can't transmit our beliefs to another person even if we want to. We can discuss and describe to the best of our ability, but ultimately spirituality is an inner journey that can't be fully communicated.

It can be helpful to understand that transition away from a faith is not something a person does on purpose, just as conversion toward a faith is not done on purpose. They both happen. Both of you deserve respect and honor for your individual thoughts, feelings, and experiences -- and for what meaning you each make from your experiences.

Find your common ground.

Because of fear, couples experiencing faith transition often focus on their differences. Doing so causes anxiety and disconnection. We're hard wired to notice differences because this ability alerted our evolutionary ancestors to danger and thus helped them survive. But your spouse is not a saber-toothed tiger, so this aspect of your wiring won't help you feel connected in your marriage. The following exercise can help as you focus together on the many ways you are still aligned.

- Separately write down everything you can think of that you currently believe in or value. Beliefs can be Mormon-specific (I believe in the restoration of the priesthood), generally religious (I believe in God), relational (I believe in the Golden Rule), or secular (I believe in the importance of education or honesty or recycling).
- Share your lists with one another.
- Discuss what you have in common.

Keep your lists handy and focus on common ground as often as you can. This practice will ground you as you navigate new ways forward.

Questions I have received:

What are the best ways to overcome fear when changes are in progress?

Self-awareness is huge. I often coach couples to talk to each other from their feelings rather than from their anger or from a place of blame. For example, instead of saying, "I can't believe you're doing this to our family," you could say, "These changes are really scary for me. I'm afraid of what they mean for us going forward."

It's harder to get defensive when someone is sharing feelings. This is not a slam-dunk solution, but it ups the odds of helping the situation rather than making it worse.

What do you do when your spouse doesn't believe in God or Jesus anymore?

To quote Josh Smith, a member of the Facebook Mormon Mixed Faith Marriages support group, "To insist that another person remain unchanged means we do not love a human--we love a role; we love a myth; we love our own expectations."

Your spouse has the same right to their beliefs as you do. People have been successfully navigating mixed-faith marriages in all kinds of cultures and faith traditions for thousands of years. This is doable. It seems unnecessarily tragic that either belief or unbelief in God should divide couples when almost everyone believes in the principles that God generally stands for -- love, unity, and relationship.

Our morals/values homework didn't go well because I just don't hold importance on most of what he does and vice-versa. Our biggest points of contention now, three years post-transition, are raising the children with the values we each want. I'm focused on emotional health. He's focused on morality and obedience. We struggle with each other's approach. What is the best way to discuss this and come to common ground?

I try to help couples find the common *principles* that underlie each one's values. For example, many couples don't agree on whether or not to pay tithing, but they usually agree that charitable giving matters. Similarly, you might not agree on the details of the Word of Wisdom, but you likely agree on the importance of overall health.

Go as deep as you need to go to find the common denominator, then work up from there. Think of it as complex math.

After reading some of the advice you give, I think I made many mistakes in how I told my spouse about my faith transition. I'm not sure how to forgive myself.

There is no way you could have known how to best deal with a faith transition because in Mormonism it's not something you've been taught anything about. It's kind of like when I teach clients information they didn't know about sex. It's good to have a lot of compassion for our younger, less-informed selves. Usually we do the best we can with what we know. It's no wonder we make lots of mistakes when resources and correct information are not forthcoming.

Unfortunately, the church offers minimal help in this area. In fact, leaders have said many things over many decades that encourage division. Thus you need to be compassionate toward yourself. Accept that if you had known better, you would have done better.

How should we deal with feelings of betrayal? As a convert, I have huge feelings of feeling betrayed by the church in that almost everything I was taught is not true. And when I try to share this with my husband, it seems to bounce off of him or he just has nothing to say, and this makes me lump him in with those who I can't trust. I thought my husband would want to seek after truth, but he just seems so different than the person I thought he would be, and I guess in some ways I am disappointed in his lack of desire or focus to live life with transparency and truth. It is a huge problem for me. It feels like he wants to live with blinders on, when I have torn them off and want to explore the world around me. How can two such different world views coexist?

I agree that this is a rough place to be. At the same time, if you even imply to your spouse that "if you don't see it the way I see it, it means you too are betraying me," you're putting your partner into a really tough spot. I encourage you to switch roles and see if you would be comfortable being on the receiving end of that message.

To be more specific, suppose your husband was thinking this about you: *I thought my wife would want to seek after spiritual enlightenment and truth, which I find through prayer and scripture study. These are things she's no longer willing to do with me. How else can I feel but betrayed? She filters her information through entities I can't trust, entities that are harming our family unit. How can I trust her when she's in the same category as these untrustworthy sources?*

Try turning these ideas around and seeing the same information from your wife's perspective. This role reversal can be powerful in developing empathy and in reconnecting.

The YES/AND approach can also be powerful. Can we embrace both options on the table as mattering? Is it possible for only me to feel betrayed by the church AND see that now both of us are forced to have a different experience with the church? Can I honor the betrayal/hurt one of us experiences AND honor the edification/joy the other experiences? Can we come to a place where both of our feelings matter?

It takes time, practice, and perspective for couples to create a safe place for each partner to really see the other side and honor it. Because of the wiring we all deal with, it's super hard to not fall into the either/or position of "if I validate your position then somehow I'm diminishing my own position." But it can be done.

Should we get professional help?

I think professional help is generally not sought early enough or often enough. Professionals are especially important when a couple finds it difficult to summon hope that their marriage can survive. A competent and caring professional will help couples do work around their issues to better understand all of their options, to discern the roles they themselves play in conflict and dissatisfaction, and to practice reframes that can give new meaning and energy to places that seemed stuck. Not all mixed-faith couples should stay married, but even in situations where couples are divorcing, they will leave much less wreckage in their wake if they do this work first.

It is important to select professionals who have expertise in faith transition and who do not use their own religiousness (or lack of it) as a harmful bias for the couple. I helped found the Mormon Mental Health Association specifically because of these concerns. Providers listed on the website (www.mormonmentalhealthassoc.org) have been vetted to make sure they will deal with these matters ethically.

The way you listed phrases you typically hear from each side was pretty helpful for me. My husband doesn't talk much, and it's hard to guess what he might be thinking/feeling. Whenever I ask him what he's feeling he claims he's fine. I just can't imagine how someone can be so "fine" all the time, you know? Especially in a situation like this. (Seriously, how is he fine? Shouldn't he be yelling at me for ruining our eternal family or something!?) It feels off to me, insincere. Is it possible to be really upset and not consciously know it?

Many of us are fairly good at stuffing feelings. We've done an excellent job in American culture of training men in particular how to be "good" at this. At the same time, it's possible that your husband is really not that bothered by your transition. It's good to trust him to tell you his truth. Also important is making space for his processing as time goes by. It's okay to say something like, "You're a grown adult, and I want to respect you and believe you and not project my own experience onto you. At the same time, I know you well enough to realize that sharing feelings might not be your forte. So please know that I'm available if you ever want to explore things further or if something different comes up for you along the way."

You can also share your own process regarding his reaction or nonreaction, such as the following: "I'm frustrated that you don't seem more upset by all these changes I'm going through. It's hard to trust because I know if the situation were switched I'd really struggle. I think I'm projecting my own way of processing things onto you."

What are the main points that stood out to you in this chapter that might help your particular situation?

_____

_____

_____

_____

_____

_____

_____

_____

What is something you can commit to do differently moving forward?

_____

_____

_____

_____

_____

What is something you'd like to respectfully discuss with your spouse?

_____

_____

_____

_____

_____

Chapter 2
Avoid Unilateral Decisions

The second strategy is to avoid unilateral decisions. How?

Accept that none of us likes to be told what to do.

This acceptance gets tricky because pretty much since we hit our terrible two's, we resist being told what to do. When someone does tell us what to do, our independence alarm goes off, our own needs and desires take center stage, and we begin a power struggle that continues from that point on. Lovely, right?

At the same time (yes/and), we want connection and meaningful relationships. Our very lives and emotional well-being depend on them. Ironically, this fundamental need requires us to empathize and see as valid other people's needs and concerns. This dilemma creates what I call the "Me vs. We Internal Conflict" that all of us must manage every day. Just understanding that we're all consistently in this state of being is helpful for both self-compassion and partner compassion.

It's also helpful to take the time to notice and be mindful of times you find yourself in this conflicting space. Awareness goes a long way toward good self-management. As a therapist, I want to know how each client in a couple would answer the question, *"How do you typically manage this space?"* Some people tend to make their needs a lower priority than their partners' while others tend to advocate for their own needs more than their partners.' Either way the partnership is out of balance. Partnerships do best when needs are being met in a way that would be considered generally equal.

Be a team of individuals.

Marriage is a contract where two individuals come together with similar goals and outlooks for a journey headed in relatively the same direction. Many common expectations of marriage include acting as a team, forming a partnership, being on the same page, merging into one, and becoming soulmates. But the reality is that you still have two separate, distinct individuals in the room.

In our current marriage-centric relational climate, speaking up for individual needs can be seen as selfish, self-serving, inconsiderate, and harmful. Most of us don't do super well at allowing individuals in a marriage to have privacy. We don't tolerate differences of opinion very well either because they threaten to create relational wedges. Underlying most issues I see in my office is the implicit question, "When do my needs/wants/desires trump your needs/wants/desires and vice-versa?"

As the biblical story of King Solomon teaches, many situations can't be resolved by simply cutting the baby in half. It's critical that you deal with your tug-of-war scenarios in a way that balances both partnership and individual self-actualization. Learning how to create this balance is at the heart of developing differentiation skills. Differentiation means each person in a marriage knows how to tolerate difference while also staying connected. Good marriage therapy helps each partner build these skills.

Don't be a parent, teacher, or missionary in your marriage.

Adults don't want to be married to a parent, teacher, or missionary. The dynamics of these roles tend to quickly trigger terrible-twos behavior. They also pull you away from an egalitarian position with one another. (And nothing kills sexual intimacy like one of you acting like a parent, teacher, or missionary.) I teach my clients to avoid "asking for permission" language like the plague. Rather, we want to negotiate and collaborate. Negotiating might include statements like:

- I'm considering trying alcohol, and I want your feedback on what that would be like for you.
- I don't know that I can continue to with my church calling. It's having a negative impact on me. I know you might have some strong

feelings about this, so I'm coming to you before I do anything different.

- I'm wondering how I can be supportive of you when and if I decide to stop wearing garments.
- Is there a way we can compromise on this particular issue so that some parts of it stay the same while others change to honor better where I'm currently at?

And on the receiving end:

- I'm concerned that what you're considering might be a dealbreaker for our marriage. It's not that I'm issuing an ultimatum, but I honestly don't think that will work for me, even though I can see that it's important to you.
- I'm uncomfortable with you wanting to try that.
- Since I'm uncomfortable with this new direction you want to go in, would you be willing to give me a few days/weeks/months to adjust to the idea of it before we actually do anything about it?
- Can we try it the way you're suggesting but for a trial period? That would help me feel like it's not necessarily a final decision.
- Since we're going to lean in your direction on this topic, can we lean in my direction on this other theme?

All these statements are much more likely to preserve the feeling of partnership in your marriage than statements like, "No, I forbid you to do that" or "Yes, I give you permission to do that."

Secrecy is a unilateral decision.

Secrecy is inherently a unilateral decision. I know it can be very difficult to be honest with a partner who has communicated (directly or indirectly) that you have to choose between authenticity and the potential dissolution of your marriage. So I understand why secrecy is so common, and I'm never judgmental about it. In fact, in some cases the ethics are so complex that secrecy may be the safest, best option for a time. This is true especially in our Mormon culture, which has not helped people develop skills to manage faith transitions effectively and collaboratively. At the same time, it's good to be aware that secrecy is a unilateral decision.

Consider "Cyclical Safety."

The concept I call cyclical safety means that when I risk telling you something difficult and I know you're probably going to react in a way I'm not comfortable with, I nevertheless stay engaged instead of retreating. This is not just, "Are you a safe place for me to come confide in you?" It's also, "Am I a safe place for you to be able to react to the difficult thoughts and feelings I'm disclosing to you?"

For those of us who want honesty in our relationships, here's a good question to ask ourselves: *"What am I doing to make sure I create enough safety in the environment between us for honesty to flourish? Am I helping on this front or hurting?"*

When we've been hurtful, repair attempts are healing. For example, you might say, "I'm sorry I reacted so negatively when you were trying to share something with me. I'm not going to lie; this is really difficult for me to listen to. But I want to listen because you matter so much to me, and so does everything you're thinking/experiencing."

Consider "Systemic Authenticity."

I often joke that there's nothing "authentic" about changing poopy diapers. So why did I change thousands of them over the course of the last 20 years? Because there was something very authentic about the bigger picture, "the system," of being a parent and an aunt. If you're struggling to feel authentic doing something you don't want to do, it can help to see the behavior from the perspective of a larger system you value.

For example, a husband might continue wearing his garments because he knows the meaning doing so holds for his wife, and he's comfortable reframing the meaning of that behavior in his own mind to an act of love and commitment *to his wife*, not to his religion. A wife who deeply values attending church might decide that twice a month going on a nature walk with her husband and kids instead of church is systemically authentic. That is, she values her family system so deeply that honoring her husband's spirituality and his role as a co-spiritual leader in their home means her decision is consonant with her values.

When individuals in a marriage are making decisions about Mormon markers, such as wearing garments, holding family scripture study, and attending church, I encourage them to use a 1 to 10 scale, with a 1-level marker causing very low discomfort and a 10 causing extreme discomfort. If wearing garments triggers panic attacks, then that's a 10 on my discomfort scale. Maybe that marker is one where personal authenticity should trump systemic authenticity. If having a coffee maker on our kitchen counter is annoying and causes me worry from time to time about what the neighbors will think, maybe that's a 4 on my discomfort scale, and I can offer systemic authenticity.

Avoid coercion, exploitation, and manipulation.

You know that coercion, exploitation, and manipulation to get your way in sex is damaging to your marriage. It's also damaging in every other facet of your marriage. If your anxiety is so high about your spouse's faith journey that you use these types of methods to compel compliance and thus lessen your discomfort and tension, you need professional help. Battling these dynamics requires self-awareness, critical thinking skills, and humility. It's not good to go into the battle alone.

Often we don't want to or don't know how to recognize that we're employing these tactics in our relationship. Being open to examining our own ways of contributing to dysfunction and being willing to see them is important. It's easy to see that a partner who inflicts physical wounds to compel compliance has crossed a boundary, but breach of emotional boundaries can be harder to discern. Most of us would be surprised to know that we can be more abusive and toxic than we would ever want to admit.

Questions I have received:

The problem we have is communicating our feelings about the church in a way that doesn't feel like an attack on the other one. We attend different churches, and I'm the active Mormon. Almost every time my husband wants to talk about his doubts, I perceive it as an attack and feel like my faith is under attack. We want to be open with each other with our feelings, but we usually don't do it well.

This is such a common experience and exactly the scenario where differentiation skills come in. We tend to tie agreement and conformity to loyalty and togetherness, but conformity despite underlying feelings equals sameness. Fake agreement creates a false sense of intimacy, not true intimacy. It's also often easier to go along to get along. But genuine intimacy is about staying connected while having full awareness of differences. It's tough to stay truly present and curious for your partner when your anxiety is rising. But doing so builds intimacy. As you practice your differentiation skills, working hard to be self-aware and to honor differences while staying connected, you'll get better at it.

What are the main points that stood out to you in this chapter that might help your particular situation?

_____

_____

_____

_____

_____

What is something you can commit to do differently moving forward?

_____

_____

_____

_____

_____

What is something you'd like to respectfully discuss with your spouse?

_____

_____

_____

_____

_____

Chapter 3

You Both Have a Right to Parent Your Children

My third strategy is to accept the idea that you both have a right to parent your children. How?

Seek education and professional help.

Although marriage is ideally focused on teamwork and partnership, nothing can bring out the claws faster than issues that trigger your inner mama bear or papa bear instincts. It's normal to feel upset, defensive, and protective when you're in conflict with your partner about your kids. But normal doesn't necessarily mean okay or beneficial. Unfortunately, statistics show that parenting disputes play a major role in many divorces.

Whether you stay together or divorce, you'll have to co-parent. So it's in your best interest, and definitely in your children's best interest, to figure out how to co-parent effectively. Kids do better with less parental conflict, and that fact doesn't change with marital status. Your kids need you to figure this out.

Aside from the education I offer in this chapter, you can learn better parenting skills by taking classes (online or in person), reading books separately or together, consulting reputable websites, and getting professional help.

Practice self-compassion and partner compassion.

When you're early on in a Mormon mixed-faith marriage, the parenting setting will likely be your most difficult and pressing challenge. You'll face discussions and decisions that many of your peers don't face. For those who fit the mold, Mormonism does a good job of creating a fairly family-friendly structure that you can easily plug into. The community creates a timeline for your children that you simply follow -- Primary, the Young Women or Young Men program, seminary, dating and sexual behavior instruction, missions, BYU education, and temple marriage. When both parents are believers, they feel the church structure supports them well as they raise their kids.

By contrast, in families where one parent is in faith transition, the believing parent usually feels profound fear that the church structure might no longer serve as a safety net for their family. Conversely, the transitioner often feels profound fear that their kids will be influenced by a system that now undermines their authority and "worthiness" status.

This situation is super tough for both of you. It's okay to just sit with that reality for a bit and practice compassion for your spouse's feelings and for your own.

Understand where privilege lies.

Within the church system, a believing spouse experiences privilege that an unbelieving spouse does not. The way Mormons typically talk about doubters and disbelievers in church settings is quite negative and even hostile. Parental authority is often undermined as inactive or unbelieving parents are treated as "less than." Some transitioning parents are explicitly told by leaders that they're no longer worthy. Others are disciplined by removal of temple privileges and released from callings. Many fathers are forbidden to participate in religious rituals, such as baptism, confirmation, and priesthood ordination. If a father chooses not to participate because doing so feels disingenuous, he's likely to be shamed about that decision. Sometimes children are encouraged to become missionaries to their doubting parent or to be a "good example," creating disrespect toward the parent.

I encourage parents in mixed-faith families to present a united front to their ward community. This takes time to figure out and includes issues such as not allowing the transitioning parent to be disrespected in front of the children, talking to Primary teachers when lessons will include stories about inactive parents, bringing to the bishop's attention insensitive messages given over the pulpit, and agreeing to defend one another in social settings where one or the other might be disparaged.

In some cases, depending on where you live, the transitioning spouse might experience privilege and the believer belittling. Religious folks may be dismissed as brainwashed, uneducated, or naive. It's just as important to defend the believing spouse and set appropriate boundaries if they are facing undermining by friends, family members, or community members.

Apply the golden rule.

Don't expect your spouse to stay silent about their beliefs or ideas in any way that you would not want to be silenced yourself. Although the transitioner is the one changing the contract, it is not sustainable for either parent to keep the other from teaching their truth to their children and or from bringing their authentic selves to the parent-child relationship. To expect anything different is a form of emotional abuse. Unfortunately, I often see this attempt to control on both sides of the faith transition dance. Transitioners are told they can't talk to their kids about their new beliefs, and believers are told they can't teach their kids the gospel.

Whether we like it or not, unless the other parent of our children has died, we're parenting with another living, breathing, fully dimensional human being. Unless abuse or other forms of criminality are part of the equation, not liking your partner's ideas is not going to cut it as a reason to keep them from parenting your children.

This is not to say we make changes quickly in our parenting. It's always healthier to make changes in family dynamics slowly, transparently, and age-appropriately.

Make sure both of you are both a "spiritual" and a "secular" leader in your home.

I often see dynamics where the believing spouse now runs all Family Home Evenings, family prayers, scripture study, etc., while the transitioner focuses on all things rational and historical. Figure out ways to expand the concept of educational and spiritual opportunities within your home. Transitioning parents are moral, ethical beings with lots of potential to bring new perspectives that can strengthen your family. Believing parents are educated, complex beings who should not be defined only by their religious beliefs.

For example, I've seen couples take turns for devotional family time. The believer says traditional Mormon prayers while the transitioner leads meditation. I know of parents who include in their definition of scripture study both the standard works and non-Mormon literature.

Going back to the values exercise I spoke of in Chapter 1, remember that you still agree on many things. Focus on common-ground topics for family home evenings. Consider contracting with one another to occasionally represent the point of view that usually the other one would express. For example, the believer can on occasion initiate discussion about historical issues that were represented inaccurately at church. The transitioner can bring up traditional Mormon ideas that they agree with and find edifying. Don't play just one role. You'll bore yourselves and your kids too.

Have your partner's back.

There is no reason why both of you can't speak your truth within the family system AND represent your partner's perspective. Here's a very simple example: "For me, Joseph Smith was a charismatic person who played an important role in American history as a leader of a church he created. For your mom/dad, Joseph Smith is a prophet who received messages and authority from God. It's okay that we each have our own take on this. Over time you'll figure out what you believe for yourself. Both of us will support you in that process."

Avoid guilt trips.

You might be doling out guilt to your children consciously, and you might also guilt them subconsciously. Avoid causing your children to feel like you're testing their loyalty. This can happen when you express disappointment that they seem to be leaning in your transitioning spouse's direction. It can also happen if you act elated when they lean toward your believing perspective. And vice-versa. I would hope that everyone wants their children's spirituality to develop outside of a guilt trip.

Can you be differentiated enough to celebrate your child's thoughts and ideas regardless of whether they reflect your own? Can you trust your children to take their own spiritual journeys? Can you accept that their journeys will be different and that each one's carefully made choices are in their best interest? Ironically, there is something profoundly Mormon about taking this approach. After all, according to Mormon doctrine, Heavenly Father's parenting style holds personal agency sacred while Satan's approach is to compel everyone to conform and obey.

Give your children permission to have both concerns AND spiritual experiences.

Often I see kids within a Mormon context being taught doctrine and practice in ways that make it very difficult for them to know how to express disagreement. I also see kids taught secular ideas without being offered avenues to express spiritual experiences.

My husband and I have developed a ritual around this issue that I really enjoy. Either in the car on our way home from church or while gathered around the dinner table, one of us will ask each child to share something they learned at church that they enjoyed, agreed with, or "felt the spirit" or "felt enlightened" about AND something they didn't enjoy, disagreed with, or felt uncomfortable about. We do this ourselves too.

We've found this approach is an excellent way for our children to get the message that they are the authority on their own experiences, that they can trust themselves, and that there are many ways to "mormon."

See mixed-faith parenting as an asset.

As hard as mixed-faith parenting can be, its positives outweigh any negatives once you surmount initial hurdles. Children from mixed-faith homes benefit tremendously when they see parents who manage differences in emotionally regulated ways. They come to understand the complexities of different people having different positions and thus begin building their differentiation skills early on. They have more empathy for others and their variety of opinions. They develop better critical thinking skills.

As the two of you model negotiations effectively, your children will feel safe having their own opinions and beliefs and sharing them with you. This sharing strengthens your relationship and decreases secrecy, which ups the risk of many harmful outcomes. Also, their friends will feel safe to share their beliefs and opinions when they're in your home.

With the direction statistics are trending, it's becoming more likely that your children will be in a mixed-faith marriage or parenting relationship themselves. What better gift can you offer them than to model and teach family unity and cohesiveness in a mixed-faith context?

Question I have received:

How do we know what's age-appropriate in regards to controversial subjects? For example, we've already told our children that there are multiple versions of the First Vision and that people believe different things about church teachings. We've tried simplifying information, but how do we know what's appropriate and what's too complicated for their young minds? Our kids are ages 9, 7, almost 5, and 20 months.

Simple narratives at these ages are perfectly appropriate. At about pre-adolescence (starting about age 8), you can take it up a notch and at teen years up another notch.

It's also helpful to follow your children's lead. What questions do they have? When you talk to them about a topic, do they act bored or even interested at all? If you tell your 9-year-old that Joseph Smith had more than one wife, for example, and she asks some pretty sophisticated questions, go ahead and answer them (just not PhD style). She might get it quickly and want more, so give her more. A 15-year-old to whom you offer the same information might give you a deer-in-the-headlights look, so you stop. Again, follow their lead.

What are the main points that stood out to you in this chapter that might help your particular situation?

_____

_____

_____

_____

_____

What is something you can commit to do differently moving forward?

_____

_____

_____

_____

_____

What is something you'd like to respectfully discuss with your spouse?

_____

_____

_____

_____

_____

Chapter 4
Consider Anger Management and Displaced Anger

My fourth strategy is to consider anger management and watch for displaced anger. What and how?

We all have a right to the feeling of anger.

If you've watched the movie *Inside Out,* you've seen anger personified as the cute little red guy. He's not that scary, right? After all, anger is only a feeling and a secondary feeling at that (meaning it has a primary emotion beneath it, usually fear, pain, or sadness).

If you haven't watched *Inside Out,* watch it with your kids! It's a great education in emotional intelligence.

Actually, anger can be scary, and why we tend to push it outside the realm of legitimate emotion and try to get rid of it as quickly as possible. But like all feelings, anger has a right to exist. And there are justifiable reasons to be angry. Even Jesus, Christianity's example of perfection, showed anger, albeit "righteous" anger. He has a fit with those who disrespected sacred space.

Well, faith transitioners are angry. Their sacred spaces of identity, assumed truth, community, and upbringings have been disrespected. Believing spouses are angry. Their sacred spaces of home, testimony, and life expectations have been disrespected. We are all throwing righteous fits -- and with good reasons. Let's be willing to acknowledge our anger and the good reasons for it. Let's start there.

Recognize that we are not typically comfortable with anger.

Mormonism generally is not a culture that's comfortable with anger. We're taught that "contention is of the devil." Interpersonal tension and anger are seen as sin, to be highly controlled and packed away. So when faced with these normal feelings, we're ill-equipped to manage them. We sweep them under the rug, which makes us conflict-avoidant and/or passive-aggressive instead of direct. Because we're so conditioned to be nice and to be seen as nice, we "protect" each other from the truth rather than cause conflict. This approach creates distance rather than connection, which actually conflict can promote if it's handled well. Avoiding conflict often results in protection-style marriages instead of intimacy-style marriages.

So, anger in our culture tends to be ignored, dismissed, shelved, or shamed. And how do we feel when we are ignored, dismissed, shelved, or shamed? ANGRY! Can you really blame anger if it comes back to bite you in the butt every time it's not addressed?

Anger is a great informant.

The whole point of the movie *Inside Out* is that each feeling has its role. A job. A reason for existing. Anger is a great information giver. It can clue you in to ways you're being mistreated or things that are not fair. It can offer you insights you wouldn't otherwise have considered. If you're willing to notice patterns of anger, you might start to better understand things that trigger you, things that are not healthy for you to be a part of, and messages that have shaming effects on you.

Anger is a great motivator.

Often we're not moved to action about something that needs attention until we feel the motivation driven by anger. We're creatures that resist change. Change is hard -- even positive change. Anger sometimes presents us with the last straw that makes our status-quo no longer okay. So, anger can act as a catalyst that gets us moving away from behavior patterns or relationships that have become toxic for us. Healthy boundaries are a great product of anger. Embrace this reality.

Anger is an important part of the grief cycle.

Faith transitions are chock full of grief for everyone involved. It stands to reason that each spouse is going through their own version of the grief cycle. Feeling anger is not only a normal part of this process but also a necessary part, a part that, if acknowledged and valued, can help you heal rather than detract from your healing. Lean in to your anger, not away from it.

Anger has consequences.

While anger has its upsides, it also has downsides. Anger primarily functions in what is commonly referred to as our reptile brain. Yup, the reptile brain is pretty much what you're visualizing – tiny. Anger is a survival mechanism that triggers our defense responses – flight, fight, or freeze. These responses can be initiated in nanoseconds, increasing your adrenaline, diverting blood away from your brain to your extremities, and temporarily lowering your IQ. Yup. You're usually stupider when you're angry. Sorry to break it to you.

Because we act stupider when angry, over time unmanaged anger can have a huge negative impact on the relationships we care most about. Even if your anger is "righteous," you're going to have to figure out a way to manage it if you expect people you care about to stay engaged with you. In worst case scenarios, anger can become violent. Violence can never be seen as acceptable.

Unchecked, anger can be paralyzing.

Getting stuck in anger can color your view of the world by placing too much importance on only certain parts of your experiences. Therapists call this lopsided focus "hyper-vigilance" or "confirmation bias." You pay attention only to the things that confirm what you're angry about. Hyper-vigilance can play a role in developing or exacerbating mental health disorders, such as clinical depression and anxiety. And it distorts your reality.

Like all feelings, anger can lie to you.

Most of us hugely underestimate the effect emotions have on our choices and insist we're being rational. But each and every one of us is primarily an emotional creature. Confirmation bias is real. It doesn't matter how smart or rational you think you are, you're affected by it. This is true of believers and non-believers alike. While critical thinking hopefully comes into play as well, we can never be purely critical thinkers. If you're interested in learning more about this, check out the book *The Righteous Mind: Why Good People Are Divided by Politics and Religion,* by Jonathan Haidt. Another resource is the Mormon Mental Health Podcast, which has several episodes that address this issue.

Anger likes the blame game.

Instead of focusing on ourselves and how anger could be informing us, it's far easier to displace our anger onto our spouse, the church, what is thought of as anti-Mormon literature, the podcast you just listened to, your parents, your entire upbringing, etc. Be cautious about anger's tendency to turn into a blame game where you deflect responsibility for your life away from yourself. Anger can also lead you to resist seeing the full picture of your life and its many layers.

Anger likes "either/or" scenarios.

Anger hates the "yes/and" approach because it forces anger to become nuanced. Nuanced anger is usually more tepid than either/or anger. It's not as powerful or seemingly justifiable in the way either/or anger can be.

Black and white thinking is common in both American and Mormon culture. Whether you're the believer or the transitioner, you will benefit from self-awareness work in this area.

Balance anger in your life.

A faith transition can be life consuming. After all, it hits you at the very core of your identity. At the same time, it doesn't have to define you. Look for ways to find more balance in your life. If you love podcasts but can't name a recent podcast you've listened to that isn't about Mormonism, it might be time to diversify. If you're a scripture reader but can't tell me something of note you've read that isn't published by Deseret Book, it might be time to diversify.

Don't stay stuck. Step into new territory. Look for other themes. Figure out what you value outside of faith issues and move toward those spaces. Put a portion of your energy into other things.

Find safe ways and places to process anger.

If possible, make your spouse one of your safe places to process anger. Clueing each other in to your innermost feelings increases emotional intimacy and builds closeness. But don't rely solely on your spouse. Doing so is likely to overburden the relationship. If both of you consistently fall into toxic conflict when you try to be a safe space for each other, you'll need to step away from using your spouse for this purpose. And find a good marriage therapist.

Safe spaces also include support groups, friends, and family members who know how not to fuel your anger. Venting can be helpful to a point, but mostly use your resources to move toward solutions. For books, I recommend *The Dance of Anger*, by Harriet Lerner. Even though it's directed primarily to a female audience, it can benefit any reader.

Create boundaries for your anger.

It's helpful to decide on set times or ways that you allow anger to show up. For example, at set times of the day or week, sit with your anger in a meditative way. Practice non-judgment as you experience anger, doing a body check to see what your physiology is telling you about your angry feelings.

You also need strategies for telling anger you need a break. To take your mind off angry feelings, consider taking a shower, watching a TV show, having sex, or playing with your kids.

Angry sex, done right, can be a lot of fun.

Just a side tip from your friendly sex therapist: As long as you're following the principles of sexual health (consent, non-exploitation, honesty, and mutual pleasure), angry sex can be hot, passionate, stress-relieving, and a lot of fun.

What are the main points that stood out to you in this chapter that might help your particular situation?

_____

_____

_____

_____

_____

_____

_____

_____

_____

_____

What is something you can commit to do differently moving forward?

_____

_____

_____

_____

_____

_____

_____

_____

_____

_____

_____

_____

_____

_____

What is something you'd like to respectfully discuss with your spouse?

Chapter 5
See Your Mixed-Faith Marriage as an Asset

My fifth strategy is to be willing to see your mixed-faith marriage as an asset instead of a liability. How?

Be intentional about this reframe.

Before you read any of my next points, make a conscious decision that you're willing to reframe your relationship in this way. Say something to yourself like the following: "Yes, I'm willing to see my mixed-faith marriage from the perspective of a gift or opportunity rather than a wedge or divider."

If you can let this idea sink in, the next time you're faced with a mixed-faith issue, you'll be better equipped to stay calm and find solutions. The problems don't have to define your entire relationship, and they don't have to carry more meaning or power than they deserve.

Don't assume same-faith marriages are any more emotionally intimate than yours.

When I work with spouses where both are either believing or both are non-believing, they don't typically know much about the intricacies of each other's values, ethics, morals, and dreams. Sometimes spouses make a lot of assumptions about one another that aren't true. If a spouse says, "We're Mormon," I ask him or her to explore what, exactly, that means. If a spouse says, "We're agnostic," I ask the same question. Often the answer surprises the other spouse.

One of the gifts of mixed-faith dynamics is that you're forced to step into an in-depth space of curiosity and understanding (if you're willing). Many marriages don't take the opportunity to inhabit this emotionally rich and intimate space. When done well, this exploration will strengthen your intimacy as a couple. You come to know more about each other than you ever did before. Each of you becomes confident that you're willing to continue learning about the other as changes happen throughout your lives together. This willingness builds trust, especially when you realize that your partner will stick with you even after being corrected on his or her errant assumptions about you.

Working out differences and still feeling that you have each other's backs lies at the heart of intimacy. Sameness is easy for those willing to fake agreement, but it will fool you into false intimacy every time.

Intentionality around spirituality is a potential benefit.

Just as curiosity and leaning in to a partner who no longer believes can increase intimacy, they can also deepen spirituality. In a mixed-faith partnership, each of you has to sit with your beliefs and values in new ways. Neither of you can operate on auto-pilot any longer. You have to make conscious choices about how to engage one another, how to negotiate your parenting styles, and how to get creative about inclusive rituals and lifestyle decisions. These opportunities offer the potential for a more dimensional marriage than is possible for those who stay in comfortable routines.

Though going off auto-pilot initially can be painful, your new intentionality will lead to reclaiming your adult authority. It's developmentally appropriate to do this. I believe too many in Mormonism stay in an adolescent stage of development, with the church as a chronic parent. It's ironic that the uniquely Mormon invitation to become like God -- and a peer and a friend to God -- gets lost in an authority-oriented culture that tends to infantilize.

Allow your partner to influence you.

Marriage researcher John Gottman has found that in strong marriages, both spouses allow the other to influence them. In his book *The Seven Principles for Making Marriage Work*, Gottman says that allowing your partner to influence you offers you the gift of another perspective that you could never access on your own. Yes, it can be scary, annoying, and/or confusing to be given information you're not comfortable with (on either side of the spectrum of belief). But new perspectives shared by your spouse give you an ongoing opportunity for growth and enlightenment as you stretch yourself through points of discomfort.

A mixed-faith home can be an asset to your children.

As I discussed in the parenting chapter, if you have children, your mixed-faith marriage gives you a situation that most parents never experience. You have a tremendous opportunity to model inclusion and respect for the choices of others. The children I've seen come out of these mixed-faith environments are generally compassionate, smart, humorous, open, and critical thinkers who don't take themselves too seriously. They are better equipped than many of their peers to face similar dynamics with friends, partners, and colleagues.

Adam and Eve had a mixed-faith marriage.

When you think about it, there's nothing more Mormon than a mixed-faith marriage. It's the story of Adam and Eve. Eve chose knowledge and experience that separated her from Adam for a time, and we don't damn her for that in our tradition. Adam chose his partner over the comfort, structure, and godliness of the Garden. They faced the world together, in a different relationship with deity and the earth than they had been accustomed to.

Yes, they faced difficulties they might not have had if the story had been different. And yet we honor their choices as inspired, good, and even necessary. Their faith transition is at the heart of the entire reason Mormons believe we are here -- to know pain so we can experience its opposite, joy. Whether for you this story is literal, symbolic, or something in between, it includes beautiful concepts you can apply to your life.

Embrace your status as a mixed-faith couple. Let it become one of your greatest strengths. Even if you eventually separate or divorce, whatever you learn from the situation will be a valuable part of your journey. Your growth from this specific circumstance can influence for good your development into the person you will be a year from now or five years from now and beyond.

May you experience peace, comfort, growth, and intimacy you never could have imagined before facing this "trial."

What are the main points that stood out to you in this chapter that might help your particular situation?

_____

_____

_____

_____

_____

What is something you can commit to do differently moving forward?

_____

_____

_____

_____

_____

What is something you'd like to respectfully discuss with your spouse?

_____

_____

_____

_____

_____

Made in the USA
Lexington, KY
05 November 2019